Don't Get Hooked on a Feelin'!

BECOME THE SALESPERSON YOU CHOOSE TO BE

By: Teresa Lynn

Featuring: Frank Eppolitio
Editor: Karlie Saumier

www.gatheredbooks.com

INTRODUCTION

Living your dreams should be non-negotiable!

What are your dreams? Besides generalized statements such as, "I want success and money." What do you dream of accomplishing in this life? Are you a salesperson? Have you intentionally created your sales identity? Who are you as a salesperson? **Will you develop your sales identity and live your dreams?** You can only live your dreams or meet your goals if you know what they are and who you are.

Dreams or goals can be something you create from your passion, practicality, or faith. Regardless of where the goals are coming from, you are only able to fight for them if you clearly articulate what you are dreaming about. Your dreams and vision reflect your identity. Often, your dreams change as you grow. That is okay. You still need to know what you are working toward. Do more than talk about your dreams and goals. Remember, "All hard work

brings a profit, but mere talk leads only to poverty."
Proverbs 14: 23, NIV

Our careers become an integral part of our identity. If you are a doctor, nurse, pastor, or teacher, those titles aren't simply what you do. The titles are also a part of who you are. The same is true for salespeople. Our trade is a part of our identity. We may get caught up in the sales game and get hooked on a feelin'. The need for the "high" can sabotage the salesperson we want to be and the dreams we are chasing.

There are many of you seasoned sales professionals who will relate to what I share in this book. Most of you have thought about it but may not know how to express it. How do you teach sales identity? Learning or teaching systems and sales processes is easy enough. How do you teach what is beyond soft skills? What do you wish people knew about sales?

A sales manager got caught off-guard when the sales team asked:

- "Will you teach us more about sales?"
- "We don't feel like we know enough about sales."
- "Will you do more sales training for the teams?"

These questions should not have been a surprise. Many of the team members are launching their careers. Others have been in sales, but not in that industry. Some have years of experience but need to learn technology-aided selling. There are even some with industry experience who could use retraining. Their previous training consisted of the following:

- "Here is how you log in."
- "When someone calls, say this, do that. Here is a script. Use it if you need anything."

They were trained to take orders, like ordering Door Dash, rather than being enabled to become sales professionals. It is as Zig Ziglar often said:

"Great salespeople are not born. They are made."

The sales team wanted to grow. What is most important for a sales team to learn about sales? The manager gave it much thought and brought the question to me. My answer to the question was simple, everything! I want them to know all I've learned in my twenty-plus years in sales. I want them to know all the latest ways technology can and will help them. I want them to know everything my coaches and mentors taught me. I want them to learn and understand every word Zig Ziglar ever spoke. I want them to see the fun they can have, the money they can make, and the pitfalls to avoid. I want them to know that they can become the salesperson they choose to be.

There are many tips, tricks, and qualities to develop. I want them to know it all! I want to know it all too. You must be a willing life-long learner. We will never know it all, but we must never stop desiring knowledge.

Sales professionals must develop their own unique sales identity and style. Your character and sales identity are part of the essence that makes you, you. Your sales identity helps to build your value. Zig Ziglar knew that how you value yourself is important "… develop a strong sense of your value as a salesperson, recommends Ziglar." (Ziglar, Secrets of Closing a Sale)

How do you equip your team to become great sales professionals? How do you teach them to be phenomenal? How do you teach interdependence? Is your mind swirling? Where do we start?

This book is a start or restart, depending on your circumstances.

People usually teach by using what they know. So, I will start with what I know. The two thing things that I know the most about are:

1. Sales And
2. The Bible

I was raised in the church and often use the Bible to work through my thought processes. I also have a degree in religion. If you are not religious, churchgoing, or a Jesus-following kind of person – do not worry. You are not getting a sermon. The Bible is considered Hebrew Wisdom Literature, so it is in that way that I will make references.

How do salespeople become great? It is by doing one thing at a time. Knowledge layering is a Bible concept. The Bible says, "…precept upon precept, line upon line…," (Bible Gateway, n.d., pp. IS 28:13, KJV) The answer to how to build great salespeople is by creating a solid foundation and then adding one thing at a time.

Most of us have seen a construction site. The thing about construction is before anyone can lay a foundation, the area is excavated or prepared. Our minds are the foundation for everything that we do in sales. Our thoughts can help us achieve the impossible or convince us to give up.

This book will help to prepare our minds as the foundation of our sales careers. It will help salespersons of all levels (managers, too) refresh and energize their efforts. The game is changing, and we must be 'in the know.' We need to find a way to "break ankles," as they say in basketball. (No ankles are literally broken.) We all need as much motivation as we can get. Zig would say, "Motivation does not last, but neither does bathing. That is why we recommend it daily." You may notice that I reference the late Zig Ziglar frequently. I absorbed the words of Mr. Ziglar in my formative years. I learned much from Mr. Ziglar. Zig Ziglar helped me find my sales identity as I chose the salesperson I am.

I dedicate this book to my insurance family, my biological family who tolerate me and my unending projects, those who helped create this book, everyone who reads my words, all my mentors, and the family of the late Mr. Zig Ziglar. His career changed my life and countless others. I'm exponentially thankful to all these people.

Don't get hooked on a feelin'!

Become the salesperson you choose to be.

LIVING YOUR DREAMS SHOULD BE NON-NEGOTIABLE!

~ Teresa Lynn ~

Chapter 1

"GOAT"
Greatest Of All Time

Who is the greatest salesperson of all time, the GOAT? Do you think of Steve Jobs or Elon Musk? Neither? How about Mary Kay Ash, Zig Ziglar, Lee Iacocca, or P.T. Barnum? Still, no? Do you think of Wallstreet, used car sales, or car warranties? How about media, educators, or government leaders? Did you think of religious leaders? The Apostle Paul or Jesus?

The GOAT! The greatest of all time depends on the point of view or metrics. There are many factors to consider. What is the product, digital item, or service. Who is selling it, to whom are the items sold, what season are the items sold in, what is the state of the economy, and how much time did the salesperson have to sell it. What did the sale achieve?

I watched a documentary about basketball players. It provided player statistics from decades of basketball and tried to ascertain which players were the greatest. To me, the obvious answer was Michael Jordan. My bias skews my opinion. He was the player I grew up watching. Saying, "Who is the greatest?" is hard to quantify.

As it relates to basketball, I still say Michael Jordan. That will always be my truth. You may have a different reality.

My truth created a passion for both basketball and sneakers. It was an absolute to me. It drove my purchases of Jordan sneakers for a couple of decades. My son had his first pair of Jordan sneakers before he could walk. **You, your ability to sell, and your relationships will, sometimes, shape truth for others that can ignite passions and influence purchases.**

I will ask again, "Who is the GOAT?" In sales, I say Satan. (AKA Lucifer, The Devil, The

Enemy) has the most sales. Satan has the most numbers. Stay with me.

Christians make up 31.6% of the world's population. (Pew Research , 2022) That means 68.4% of people are not Christians. There are fewer Christians if you only count Evangelicals worldwide. (Do not get too deep into that comment. We are talking about sales and not debating theology. Jesus loves everyone.) The overwhelming majority of people in the world are not Christian.

By the above metrics, it would mean that Satan is the GOAT.

The Devil wins over Jesus in a landslide if you only look at numbers. **There are times when numbers do lie!** Have you ever made a deal with the Devil or a contract that felt like it came straight from hell? You made an exception or bent a few rules, and before you knew it the account was an unending headache.

How do you treat your small accounts? Do you work as hard for them as you do large accounts? Are small customers more likely to stay with you?

Do you ever get outsold by teammates who need to slow down and do things correctly? You worked hard on a small account. You did all the right things, precisely according to the process. Meanwhile, your teammate sloppily closed three sales to your one small client. Were you outsold?

Three days later, your teammate lost those sales (or spent the next week cleaning up the mess they made by not doing it right the first time.) Your one deal stayed on the books! The following week you get another sale because you don't have to chase your tail cleaning up a mess. Plus, that small account you wrote will grow and bring more business. Which of you was truly more profitable? Who outsold whom?

In the Bible, a goat is the symbol of Satan. He is the chief of all liars. Stereotypically, salespeople are referred to as lying devils. I disagree with the stereotype. Sales professionals work hard to master their craft. At times good people go wrong. There are other times when **a person's humanity causes little slips of integrity.** When you stumble, get back up! Proverbs say if you are doing right, you might fall seven times, but you will keep getting up (Proverbs 24:16). Selling is an emotion-fueled career. Learn the pitfalls so you will know how to avoid them.

Jesus has less volume than Satan. It may look like Jesus was not the GOAT. When you understand the return on investment (ROI) you know that Jesus is the Greatest of All Time. Jesus and the ROI He brings is unparalleled in this life and throughout eternity. Jesus does things right the first time and they last forever. No person who truly has a relationship with Jesus wishes they had chosen Satan. That is 100% retention! The work of Jesus creates joy and peace. There is never after-the-sale chaos or destruction. Jesus is the only place where you can get what He has to offer. Those who genuinely have taken what Jesus offers will tell others.

Do you know the story of David and Bathsheba? David, a king, is lounging on his rooftop bar. David looks down and sees this super-hot chick taking a bath outside. Bath…she..ba! The Devil said, "Go on, get her. She is lonely. Her husband is always at war. You should know. He is your soldier. The Devil continued, "He is one of your top generals. You know he will not be back for a while. Show her some love." King David falls for the lies. (We do not know if Bathsheba was trying to get the king's attention initially or not.) We do know that she fell for the lies too. The Devil told Bathsheba, "Your husband does not appreciate you. He's never here! All the time you have been married, that man has never told you how gorgeous you are when you bathe. The king himself noticed how fine you are. You better enjoy it! You deserve it. Take care of yourself." Bathsheba fell for it.

As the story goes, she got pregnant. The king needed to cover up the affair, so he tried to send Bathsheba's husband home from duty. (Do you know what I mean? He wanted Bathsheba and her husband to "be together" to say the child belonged to the husband. Trifling!)

It is one lie and then another. Finally, King David (once called a man after God's own heart) put his top general, Bathsheba's husband, on the frontline to kill him. King David then married Bathsheba. She wasn't the king's only woman. And their son – he died. (The Bible says it a little differently. I added spiritual speculation and my emphasis. If you want to read the real story: 2 Samuel 11)

David and Bathsheba bought lies from the Devil at a massive cost. Untruth is costly!

When done the way Satan would do them, sales cause nothing but trouble. When you get numbers with lies, trickery, doing things wrong, forgoing integrity, not following compliance, or disregarding clients, it leads to destruction. It may also kill your profitability. Satan's way even causes destruction when you make small moral concessions or omissions for the sake of the sale. It makes sense. In the Bible, Satan exists to kill, steal, and destroy.

Are you above a 'failure of integrity'? I doubt it. You are human. When your integrity fails, how will you recover? Will you be like King David and make it worse? Will you be honorable, own your mistake, and do your best to set things right?

Long-term profitability is optimal when you educate yourself and your clients. Do what is best for the client. People may not remember what you did for them, but they will remember how they felt about you. Customers will remember the wicked salespeople who stuck them with dishonesty. They will label salespeople based on one bad experience with a dishonest salesperson. Plus, if you have taken shortcuts, cases become headaches. They cost you more time and money in the long run. You cannot achieve long-term relationships when a client feels like your victim after the sale, and you feel like a vampire.

The Apple Lady

During the early days of my insurance career, I was a server on the weekends to supplement my income. (I started at the very, very bottom. My first insurance job paid around $6.00 per hour. I wasn't entitled to a thing, and you are not either. It is best if you are willing to do whatever it takes and willing to do it the right way. It was not much money, but it was an opportunity.)

"The Apple Lady," as I aptly called her in my mind, came in every Sunday after church. She always wanted an Apple Dumpling for dessert. One Sunday, we were swamped. I went ahead and took her dumpling out before she finished her meal. We were running low, and I knew that was her reason for coming to the restaurant. She finished eating and sat there until the other tables were gone. Ms. Apple Lady called me over to her. She said, "You forgot to charge me for my dumpling." I apologized. Then I said, "We would have never known if you had not told me. Let me cover the cost for you." She refused. She said, "Young lady, we do not do what is right because we want a reward. We do what is right because it is right." Those words have stuck with me all these years.

In sales, there are days when right and wrong are blurry. You may feel motivated to be "nicer" than usual because you want a reward. You will be tempted to do favors for clients that cross ethical borders. Hold on to Ms. Apple Lady's words, "**We do not do what is right because we want a reward. We do what is right because it is right.**"

There are many ways to measure results. Be careful of the metrics you use to determine your success. **How much did you achieve with excellence? How much did you want to achieve?**

Who is the most outstanding GOAT of a salesperson you know? Would you relate them more to Satan (Lies, lack of integrity, destruction, and control) or Jesus (love, truth, joy, and freedom)? Satan leads with fear or false promises and manipulation. Satan wants you to feel like you "must" do it. Jesus leads with freedom of choice and wisdom. Jesus educates you on what is best and lets you choose. Which type of salesperson do you want to be. You choose your sales identity with every decision you make.

Do not believe everything you hear. If you fall for whatever someone says, it will hinder your own sales identity. I worked with a person once who seemed incredible. I did not understand how this person had many more sales than me. I called them up and asked, "What is your secret? You are killin' it!" They said, "I'm walking with the Lord." They were fired a short time later for fraudulently submitting accounts. It was not "The Lord" they had been walking with.

Ultimately, what are your goals? Is your only goal money, or do you want the satisfaction of knowing you are valuable? Does it help to know that your efforts create a positive difference? It might be active or passive, but you are choosing the salesperson you become.

Chapter 2
The Salesperson You Choose to Be

Do you want to be the GOAT? The greatest salesperson of your time? Really? What would that require of you? Do you want to be the best salesperson in your company? Really? Are you willing to do what it takes? Do you know what it takes? Do you know what your next steps are? Are you sure you want to be the best? Do you have the capacity to do what it takes? If not, are you willing to acquire the skills necessary to be the best? Are you ready to put in 100%?

Many would be great sales professionals experience burnout because they aim too high. They create lofty unreasonable goals without thinking them through. Then they feel defeated when they do not hit the objective. Set clear, achievable goals that challenge you and grow from there. You should have both short and long-term goals. Please start with the end in sight but work it down to where you can pinpoint what steps you take today, tomorrow, next week, etcetera.

Selling is fun! Consider the amount of work-life balance that is important to you. It is easy to get caught up in the game and forget about the salesperson you want to be. It is easy to get hooked on a feelin'.

I started calling offices as soon as I turned eighteen to see if they were hiring. (There was no Indeed or LinkedIn at the time.) Bob Johnson Insurance in Knoxville, Tennessee, was amused by my efforts, and they gave me an interview. Eventually, I got the job! They bought into my ability to learn to do the job they were hiring me for. My role was as an administrative worker. I didn't know anything about insurance. A few months later, I wanted to sell insurance. The owners thought I needed more time. (Honestly, they were right. I was not responsible or reliable at then.) A year later, I got a job as a life insurance salesperson.

A year after, I applied at Insurance Service Group. They called me for an interview. I walked into a boardroom with the Arrowood family. I told them how amazing I would be if given a chance to be an insurance producer. They gave me a chance. They bought into my confidence. William Arrowood Jr told me, after hiring me, "I told the family if that girl is half as good as she thinks, she will be incredible."

I took a chance on myself. I pushed for what I wanted. I wanted to be a salesperson. I chose it. There are times when you must leap. It is not arrogant to take a chance on yourself!

Your Biggest Deal

The biggest deal you ever close will be the deal you make on yourself. It might be to land a job, secure vendors for your startup, or get accepted into a school program. You are selling others on the idea of you in all those instances.

Have you heard the adage, "Think it! Dream it! Be it!"? They should add, "Then do it!" to that adage. You are not going to wake up one morning and find that you are magically the best at whatever it is you are doing.

Yes, I believe in miracles. However, even the Bible had people take part in the miracles they received. In one instance, God had the people dig ditches prepare to capture the rain that would come. In another, God gave a woman oil to sell, but she had to collect containers for the oil and then she had to sell it. There was a woman named Lydia who sold luxury purple clothe. These people were not afraid to sell. Don't be afraid to sell someone on you. You have a part to play. You must make a leap of faith.

What are you worth? Research your industry. Look for salary ranges nationwide and locally. What do you bring to the table? Why would someone want you? What is fair pay for what you are willing to offer? What is fair wage for the job you will start in? What opportunities exist for growth? Don't go into selling with an entitled attitude.

I learned a lot while I was at Insurance Service Group. I started as an entry-level producer. It was fair pay based on my experience and offered room for growth. Bobbie, the owner, and matriarch of the family treated me as an apprentice.

When I first started, my office was in the back. They gave me a box of leads on paper, a phone, and a computer. Bobbie said, "Call these." So, I did. I'm good at talking to people, and I got results. **Sales are about connecting with whoever is on the other end of the communication.** (You should learn to be a connection-maker.) Bobbie returned to check on me and asked, "Did you reach anyone?"

I said, "Yes, ma'am. Here is a list of my sales."

She said, "You got sales?"

I smirked, "Yes, ma'am!"

Bobbie said, "From the old leads?!"

I smirked again, "Yes, ma'am!"

I knew I was good. Bobbie knew I was a determined, young professional with potential who needed a mentor. The next thing I knew, she moved me into her office.

Bobbie had a way of asking people things that I would not dare ask. That is when and where I learned to be assertive.

BE ASSERTIVE!

(Jesus modeled assertiveness throughout the New Testament. Ziglar teaches passion and controlling the conversation as well.) Bobbie taught me how to control the conversation while being personable. That is different than aggressive, intrusive control. Insurance Service had a large volume of leads coming in. I quickly became exceptional at closing deals.

The agency was getting ready to sell an office across town and needed a manager. I was only twenty years old. Still, I went to manage the office. I had one assistant. My assistant, Sonya, worked eight hours daily, five days per week.

There was so much work! I worked roughly twelve hours each day, six days per week because I chose to. We had leads to sell, and I wanted to make as much money as possible. I got hooked on the feelin'! I loved the rush!

It never occurred to me to ask them to hire someone else. Seriously, the thought never once crossed my mind! I liked being indispensable. I liked doing the work. I did not mind the long hours. I enjoyed what I was doing! It was nice to be the problem solver and feel indispensable. I learned fast. I also made numerous mistakes. I cut corners and took chances. It was at a time when my social life was at its peak. When salespeople get hooked on a feelin', there is often more than one thing fueling their adrenaline rush.

Fast forward a few years. I had a high-pressure workaholic sales environment at a job that I hated. I begged God for a job that enabled me to earn a living and gave me time to be present with my family. I was choosing the salesperson I wanted to become. I was learning to set boundaries and fight for work-life balance.

My sales savvy was intact, but I had a different drive or desire. I did not need to feel essential at work because I was vital at home. I needed to earn money to provide for my family. God sent me a job! It was everything that I asked for. I worked from home as an insurance producer. It was perfect! I made a living and had a flexible schedule. I did not miss my son's sporting or school events. I was enabled to do the things important to me.

Was I a good sales employee? Yes, I think so. Was I putting in 100% to give it my personal best? No. Did I get quality business? Yes. Did I perform well compared to other employees? Definitely!

Most of the time, I was either number one or two in my region. I was the salesperson I chose to be. I did not care that I didn't hold a top spot in the nation, even though I believed I could. **I was unwilling to do what it would take to be on top.**

I could work hyper-focused for a few hours and do more than some salespeople did in a week. At the time, my ego assumed I was faster than average. I have since realized that it was more likely because others were also not performing at their personal best. We were a group of sales professionals in a sales organization intentionally not doing our best. How does that make you feel? Do you think salespeople doing less than their best is common? Is that a negative or an example of an excellent work-life balance? Most of us were hitting our company's goals for production. Where is the line between insubordinate, lazy employees and those who choose a healthy work-life balance? Can a company require someone to push themselves to their limit?

Quiet Quitting

I, and others, were the salespersons we chose to be. All of us were capable. Our income reflected our choices. You always have a choice regarding the type of sales professional you are. You need to know how much you want to achieve and how much your employer expects. Clear expectations, boundaries, and transparency on both ends make life in sales sustainable and enjoyable for employers and employees.

Choosing to reach less than 100% of your fullest potential is different from quiet quitting. Quiet quitting is when you stop doing anything extra. You exist by doing the bare minimum. You check the essential boxes. **Quiet quitting is when you have checked out and only show up for a paycheck.** You are not interested or engaged. **Quiet quitting differs from 'less than your potential'** as a salesperson. Less than your potential may still be above average or more than required. Less than potential may mean sixty hours a week or going the extra mile on a highway. Quiet quitting takes the exit.

The reasons people choose "quiet quitting" mirror the reasons for mass resignations. Those reasons include extreme micromanagement. Quiet quitting is worse than quitting. (Harvard Business Review)

You must be clear with your employer about how much of yourself you will give. Are you willing to network after hours, or is that a dealbreaker? To be the best, you must do things that others do not. The employer must be transparent about what it will take for you to achieve your goals. Both you and the employer need to agree on expectations. You will be required to perform at an acceptable level. You expect that a portion of your pay is based upon performance.

In the Old Testament Bible, there was a law that you couldn't muzzle an ox when it was working in the field. In the New Testament Bible, the law gets mentioned again. The New Testament also adds that the laborer is worthy of hire. "For the scripture saith, thou shalt not muzzle the ox when he treadeth out the corn. And the laborer is worthy of his hire." 1 Timothy 5:18, ASV. The Bible said this because if the ox was muzzled it couldn't eat. The principle we glean from this is:

> **Companies**: Treat your employees well, don't silence their voice, and pay them fairly.

Work Hard

Work-life balance is helpful for a healthy life. Establishing expectations and boundaries are also important. Equally so is hard work. Do your part. You do not get a pass to be lazy, not even if you are the most talented person of all time. The Bible says, "Whatever you do, work at it with all your heart, as working for the Lord, not for human masters" Colossians 3:23, NIV

Salespeople often get hooked on a feelin' and find that they need a pick-me-up to power through. There is no middle ground. It is moving at 100% or nothing. Most of us are guilty of having a bit of caffeine, unhealthy food, or sugar to push forward. For others, it is more serious. Working Hard does not mean being so busy that you need Adderall, cocaine, or other stimulants to keep you going. It isn't good for your long-term health. The problem might not be an inability to focus as much as you need a break, a healthy meal, or rest.

Sally Sue, a friend, works harder than anyone I know. She built an exceptional company that was profitable in its first year. Sally Sue juggles her company and family with what seems like ease. People don't see that Sally Sue has a high dose of Adderall in the mornings to get her going and then needs wine or THC to relax in the evenings.

Work hard when you work, but remember you are a human. Eighteen-hour days are not something your body can sustain indefinitely.

Quiet Firing

Did you know that Quiet firing is also a thing? "While the term 'quiet quitting' dominated the conversation in 2022, another trend emerged alongside it: 'quiet firing.', which Gallup describes as 'how managers fail to adequately provide coaching, support and career development to an employee, which results in pushing the employee out of an organization." If you are a salesperson, communicate your needs to your leadership team verbally and in writing. (Iamagazine.com April 2023 page 26, Big I, Independent Agent)

Employee Monitoring

The monitoring of employees has become a game changer. Many employers can see every keystroke, hear every phone call, and have statistics for time spent doing each task. Companies can track and account for nearly every moment of an employee's time on company computers, the internet, cars, or phones. There is virtually no privacy with these types of employers. There are even some companies that spy on the personal devices and accounts of employees.

Employee tracking is a terrible thing for many. (Few perform better with strict quantification. Extreme tracking is also separate from necessary systems and processes.) Salespeople are relational creatives.

You cannot quantify the thirty extra minutes you or your salesperson spent having coffee while building relationships. You can't put a price on the time spent getting to know and building the team you count on. If every moment gets monitored, you are developing a team who checkboxes, do not think for themselves, and feel they have no freedom to create greatness. Remember, don't muzzle them or suppress their creativity. Do you think a team that feels muzzled or imprisoned will perform at their best?

To company leaders, are you prepared to have a salesforce of mediocre box checkers? You can push them hard and make them think they are never doing enough. You can set limits high, and you teach them to be workhorses. How long before the sales team burns out? There are days and times people need to be less productive. People are not wired for unending pressure. Lazy days can be good for overall productivity and creativity. Outside-of-the-box thinking often generates revenue. Lazy days can also be good for employee retention. There is a multitude of factors that contributes to the need not to be "on". Being "at work" is different than not being "on." Do you think employees will choose to endure pressure long-term?

One of the reasons many seasoned sales professionals stuck with it was the rewards and freedom that came with the ability to produce exceptional results. Why do you think so many are opting for gig or contract-type work? People are not property to be quantified constantly. The salesforce needs freedom, not the feeling of enslavement.

If you are a company that insists on extreme micromanagement, consider factoring downtime into statistics. Without the help of substances, there is no person who is always on. You cannot simply add a foosball table (or some other form of recreation) and call it freedom.   Prisons have recreation.

If you are a salesperson whose best option is to work for a micro-managing, every-second-observing employer, be honest with yourself about your position. Understand the requirements, the stress, and the monitoring. If you find that you thrive in extreme micromanagement, go for it. If you can't thrive work hard and build your resume until you can improve circumstances.

The micromanagement trend may grow. Decide what you want. Decide who you are as a salesperson. Then decide what is possible based on your industry, experience, and environment.

Life – Fast Forward

My career has had highs and lows. It was a rollercoaster with sharp peaks. It was all manageable, until it wasn't.

It became unmanageable when Life happened. I had to slow my career down. The circumstances are a whole other book. The point is that scaling back doesn't mean you are a lousy salesperson. It means you are in a different season of life.

I stopped being an agency principal and enrolled in college classes. I also started working part-time at an agency owned by a friend.

It was comfortable. Mel, the agency owner, mastered the art of creating systems and workflows.

Yes, I did throw shade on micromanagement in the previous section. There is a difference between systems, workflows, processes, and micromanagement. Everyone needs an efficient and effective way to do things.

Mel's systems brought a rhythm and ease to the job. Most of us need a certain amount of structure and even rules. It is up to you to find the right balance for yourself as the salesperson you choose to be.

As time progressed, I graduated from college, and my friend asked me to stay full-time at his agency.

Accepting the offer to stay at my friend's agency was my mistake. There are times when, as salespeople, we settle. The option in front of us is often less scary than the dream in our hearts. There is safety in what you know.

But that is the same reason it took the Biblical children of Israel forty years to enter the promised land. Settling for less than your calling is what Zig Ziglar would call "Stinkin' thinking." (Ziglar) Terri Savelle Foy often warns you not to stop seeking to achieve your dreams. Stopping short is as common for us as it was in Bible days. (Foy)

My job was fine. Except for employee-related drama and family losses. Those kinds of problems exist everywhere. What happened next is what I call the "Stalemate."

Stalemate

The stalemate is when you and the other person (or company) are each holding back from your best because you want the other to compromise a matter. At the same time, you are not arguing. You are doing your daily duties, and you are productive. It is passive-aggressive behavior. The level of engagement and effort makes the stalemate different from quiet quitting or quiet firing. We both knew the other was holding back.

This stalemate lasted two years! When we finally discussed our terms, they were in no way agreeable. Neither of us conceded.

My intent when coming on board was to be part-time and temporary. So, I resigned and ended the stalemate. Stalemate is an exhausting position for all involved. (In our case, it wasn't ugly, and our friendship remains intact. It was simple. Our visions differed and we failed to find a compromise. Plus, I was being called to write this book.)

There are times in your career when you must make tough decisions. Those decisions will be the framework for the salesperson you choose to be. And yes, standing still is a decision. If you are in a "not bad" job, it may not be the "right" job. Living your dreams is non-negotiable when you are confident in your identity as the salesperson you choose to be.

Caution: the grass is not always greener on the other side. Daily life at any job (or even in any relationship) will not always be fun. Think through all decisions. Do not make life-altering decisions based on emotions. If you are a believer, fast and pray before making a move. Commit yourself to what you are doing. (As much as is possible.) Commitment is something many salespersons, myself included struggle with. New is fun. New feeds the adrenaline rush. Day-to-day adulting lacks the energy of newness.

Life is short. Ask yourself critical questions. (Our workbook is prepared to help you work through these questions as you advance your skills.)

Side Hustle

Having a side hustle is common. Why? Do you truly want to work full-time and spend what little free time you have doing more work? Do you love the side hustle? Is it the thing you are passionate about? Is it your calling? Do you make more money doing your side hustle than you would if you invested that energy into your primary job? Why are you doing it if it is not your passion? How much is your time worth?

What is your purpose? What is your calling? Are you in a place that aligns with your values? Is the culture a culture that you want to be a part of? There will never be a perfect job that offers everything at one time and place. But there is the best role for each season of your life.

Employers, including myself, need to define expectations for employees better. We need to outline what a typical day will look like for each role in the company. Employers and managers need to appreciate that some positions do not require a superstar. Some want to avoid excess stress but will show up every day and do quality work. Those people are valuable when everyone is honest with expectations.

Understand your capacity, how much you want, and how much effort you are willing to expend to get what you want. *Living your dreams should be non-negotiable. That even applies to those of you not interested in achieving success that exceeds your comfort zone.* You are not required to have ambition at any level. Decide who you are and what you want. Be you.

It is one thing to say, "I want to be my best." It is another thing to get up at 5 AM to have quiet time (or prayer if you pray), a quick workout, and then be at the office or networking early, be on your game all day long, have meetings for lunch, and then possibly networking in the evenings, or on weekends. Are you prepared to put into action everything it takes to be your personal best every single day? What will you do for professional development, personal development, and continued growth? Is there room to grow in the company where you work?

If you genuinely want to be your best, do you have a self-care plan? If you do not have a plan, you will need one.

Sales are addictive. **It is easy to get hooked on the feelin'**. I cannot tell you the number of salespeople I know who fall into addictions beyond sales addiction. But it is a high percentage.

You may feel yourself getting caught up in the game. At some point, it is not entirely about the money. It is about the love of the game. Sales addicts get labeled as heavy drinkers and promiscuous. Sex and sales go hand in hand if you aren't careful. Psychologists explain why:

> As with any addictive behavior, such a pattern can serve as a kind of self-medication, a way of managing or avoiding depression and anxiety, and of filling the vacuum created when feelings of sadness, grief, or rage are

chronically repressed. What really motivates sexually addictive or compulsive behavior? Extraordinary sex drive? I would disagree. It is the same thing that primarily motivates any addictive behavior: Avoidance of anxiety, anger, grief, or pain. (Psychology Today)

If you are going to play the sales game, play it well. You can beat the odds if you know what you are up against. I am not discouraging anyone from a sales career. Throughout my career, God has used sales to provide a living for me. It would be deceitful if we did not address the pitfalls head-on. Avoid getting hooked by the feelin' so you can be the salesperson you choose to be. Does your spouse or partner know the pitfalls of sales? Are they able to help you remain accountable?

Don't catch the house on fire!

Your faith and your people are more important than sales. Make time for them. Ask the people you love how well you are doing at work-life balance.

When I was raising my son, I made sure to do the bulk of my networking during breakfast meetings or luncheons. I was at home most evenings.

My friend complained she was having a hard time with work-life balance. I bragged that I felt like I was juggling things well.

My son was in the room, and he laughed. I said, "Excuse me." He said, "Nothing, forget it." I said, "No, I would like to hear this." He said, "Yes, you always made me dinner. You were physically present. Mom, do you know how often you were on the phone with clients while eating? Or while you were cooking dinner? Do you remember that once you literally caught the kitchen on fire? You forgot you were cooking because you were closing a deal? You could have burned the house down because you were not paying attention.

I love you, but if you want to encourage people to have balance, they need to do more than be in the same room. They need to pay attention to the people in the room with them. I ate alone many nights because you were not present, even though we were together in the same room." (I've done better at being present during meals since then.)

My son's advice is good. I remember the day he was talking about. I could have called the client early the next morning and still gotten the sale. I enjoyed work! Being a sales professional was a part of my identity. I was the salesperson I chose to be.

You can make as much or as little money as you want. You can do things the honest way, the dishonest way, and a million variations between. It is not always black or white. There is no easy way.

Whatever way, you will become the salesperson you choose to become. Choices are often challenging. The gray area gets blurred, and it is a hard line to walk. If you stick with it, you will probably 'get hooked on a feelin' at times. The mark of a phenomenal salesperson is not the lack of failure. It is the presence of persistence. It is continually

learning and picking yourself up when you fall. You
will fall. We all fall.

You can earn an excellent living as a
salesperson and have a great life. Be intentional with
choices, honest with yourself, and transparent with
your employer(s) and employees.

Chapter 3
Sales

How do you define sales? The dictionary defines sales as 'exchanging a commodity for money or the action of selling something.' The definition is different to the phenomenal salesperson. To the phenomenal salesperson, **selling connects a need or want to the product, service, idea, system, or person that fulfills the need or want.**

Phenomenal sales occur on a large and small scale. Phenomenal selling happens when the buyer seeks out a specific company or salesperson. Amazon and Apple are two large-scale examples. Apple sells items that only they have. Amazon sells a variety of things, and allows you to easily buy almost anything.

A small-scale example is Johnson's Mill in New Tazewell, Tennessee. The business does not have a website, at least not one I could find. The feed mill first opened in 1800. People from across the region come to buy feed, quilts, or other items at the mill. It is a case of phenomenal selling because they do what they do so well that people seek them out to buy products. How amazing would it be to open your computer or storefront and know that people seek you out because your quality speaks for itself?

Another dimension to phenomenal sales is when people refer their people to you. Your reputation, relationships, and results are why you receive referrals. Connections are proud to tell others about you. "You need widgets? Call my widget people!" Social media influencers have taken referrals to a whole other level. Referrals from influencers can be powerful. Treat them with caution in the days of cancel culture. They can both help and harm your business.

The greatest compliment for a salesperson is customer loyalty. I have a client ("A") with exponential success in the last five years. When I became their representative, the business was relatively small. I worked hard for them, and we developed a relationship based on trust. Today, competing representatives frequently show up to "A's" place, trying to drive a wedge and unseat me as their agent. Competing agents want the work with "A" now that it is a flourishing company. "A" does not budge.

I'm their first call each time they build an addition, add employees, or buy a yacht. Bring value to your clients. They need to know that you are their person.

You want clients to seek you out.

We are all in sales. A doctor may need to sell the idea of preventive healthcare, medication, or corrective measures. A lawyer must convince prospective clients that their legal expertise is the way to go, then they must convince a judge or jury that they deserve justice. A server may need to sell appetizers, desserts, or specials while they convince tables they deserve the best possible tip. A person may need to sell their partner on the idea of getting married, having children, or buying a home. Whatever the case might be, we are all selling.

As sales professionals, **it is our job to fill needs and wants with our products or services**. Our ability to successfully make connections and grow relationships determines how much we earn. My friend, Allie, owns Keola Fit. It is a Christian alternative to yoga. Allie has a degree in biochemistry, a passion for healthy lifestyles, and a love of Jesus. She created the business to have flexibility while pursuing her passion. The problem was sales. How was she going to make connections to grow her business? She chose networking, attending events, and promoting her company online. It is still in its early days, but she is gaining ground. Salespersons must find a path to prospects.

The days of the stereotypical car salesperson, the pushy fake item on the sidewalk salesperson, and the predatory funeral home patron preying on vulnerable families are over. (Disclaimer: The examples chosen are because of the stereotypes that surround them. There are phenomenal salespeople in every industry, and they deserve respect.)

Knowledgeable, tech-savvy consumers are not buying nonsense, gimmicks, or fear-based purchases.

There is a car salesperson named "DayDay." He is Gen Z. He is proud of being a car salesperson. There are no games. Do you want to buy a vehicle? He has autos for sale. He often shares on social media: pictures of the cars available and the people to whom he has sold cars. DayDay's mother is a friend of mine. At times I recognize the people to whom he has sold a car. DayDay's relationships are crucial to his sales. Equally so, DayDay has the benefit of quality mentorship. At a random event, I met DayDay's manager and mentor. His mentor is a long-time professional in car sales with a proven record of success. The mentor said, "DayDay is a good kid. He works hard. If he sticks around, I will teach him everything I know." DayDay follows the proven methods that generate success and blends them with his relationships and personality.

The tech-forward generation has brought about exponential change. This change forces sales professionals to improve their ability to connect a buyer's needs and wants to products and services while being genuine. Millennials expect you to be real. They know how to educate themselves on products and services.

To have quality salespeople in whatever your industry, find a way to develop young professionals while valuing the experienced generation. Side note: In 2023, Millennials are between twenty-seven and forty-two years old. They are powerful consumers.

How does technology impact sales for your industry? In the insurance world, Big I, Independent Agent magazine, says that sales professionals need to use first-party data instead of casting the largest net possible because it can tell you which users are serious. (Big I reference, page 34: First-party data is information collected when a person views your website or apps. Big I Magazine. (2023, April. Retrieved 04 12, 2023, from https://www.iamagazine.com/ All sales are influenced by technology. I'm not praising big tech, but technology is an effective tool. Can you imagine hammering in a nail without a hammer? That is how important technology is to sales.

Sales, selling, and salesperson are not negative titles. 'I'm a sales professional should be said with pride and dignity. If you lost your integrity somewhere, go get it!

Salesmanship is the act of making connections and building relationships. To make yourself a great salesperson, you must be a knowledgeable salesperson. To be a phenomenal salesperson, you must be a likable, life-long learner who never loses your passion for helping solve problems and make connections to answers. You will also need to learn the art of networking. That is another way of saying, "The art of meeting others and developing relationships with them."

Image matters.

Salespeople usually know their image matters to others. Has anyone ever told you that the appearance of your prospects should not matter? It shouldn't.

Zimbo Paul, a security expert, assisted with a risk management seminar my agency hosted. He taught that "behavior-based profiling" is more impactful and accurate than image-based profiling. You may think, "Zimbo was talking about criminals or someone who might be sus." Yes, he was referring to people who might be problems. The principle is still accurate for sales.

Have you heard stories about people looking less than professional who salespersons ignored? Do you remember the story about the ignored farmer who wanted to pay cash? Stop with image-based bias. It is causing you to lose money. People deserve fair treatment regardless of clothing, hair, ethnicity, age, or other image-based factors. Be a kind human. You will sell more.

As a person working in sales, you can make all the money you want, but it will never feel how you think it will feel.

Making your career in sales will require you to find aspects of the work (or the things you do with your time when you are not selling) more fulfilling than the money you receive doing it. Make a positive difference.

There are times when you will win the contest, hit the goal, or be number one, and it is not only unsatisfying, but it might even cause what I call **"The sadness of success**." Giving back (to your community or a specific group that has meaning and that you are committed to) is my best answer to overcome the emotions that creep in when it doesn't feel the way you thought it would feel.

A note to the "Old Dogs," like me, if you are leading your teams from the fictional 1980s handbook of sales, stop! Open yourselves to a new spin and increased revenue. We can order cars online and use AI to write content. Consumers are not who they used to be.

Some think that one surefire way to get hiring right is exclusively hiring youth. That is a bad idea. **Blend your team with both new and experienced talent**. Let all skill and career levels have input. **Youth + Experience = Wisdom**. We need age and skill diversity as much as all other forms.

Gone are the days of throwing up as many numbers as possible to see what sticks.

As Zig says, "Work Smarter, not harder."

Chapter 4
Relationships

With whom is your most vital sales relationship? Who are your top five? Relationships are crucial to your success in sales. We are not just talking about friends and family. We are talking about all relationships and your ability to make new ones.

Business relationships and acquaintances matter. Every person you meet is valuable. We should not manage relationships based on what they can do for us. Get to know people on a human level. It goes a long way.

At a recent conference, I met Angela. I observed her. She was polite to everyone, but she went beyond being polite. She noticed at our first dinner that I prefer sparkling water. The next few mornings, she brought me sparkling water. I watched as she found a way to engage and create a relationship with all the attendees on some level. It was not pushy or rude. Angela looked for ways to connect. It is also important to note that Angela does not have the title "salesperson." Angela is an underwriter for an insurance company. We are all in sales.

"Relationships are a key to successful sales. Relationships in sales, as in life, take time. New salespeople often focus on nailing the sale and getting money. Instead of building the relationship and giving the client the option to walk away before money changes hands.

If you take time to build trust, you will find it to be the cornerstone of your relationship, the same way Christ is the cornerstone of faith for Christians. Trust is paramount.

Let's consider each sale a building block for a lifelong relationship. We will earn trust, and the bottom line will follow. It may be slow. Not every account can be quickly closed. Cover the client's needs. Trust will earn you more business in the long run." (Karlie Saumier)

Your behavior and quality of relationships will dictate how people think of you when needs arise. If you sell cars, those you have a relationship with may choose you as their salesperson. Perhaps an acquaintance knows someone who is buying and sends them your way. The adage goes, "It is not what you know, but who you know." Who you know can be positive or negative. People may like you as a person, they may even hang out with you, but do they trust you professionally?

How do you gain trust of those you know as a professional? Be mindful of how you behave in public and online. People are watching. I was once selected because the person observed me picking up a piece of trash someone dropped in public and throwing it away. I never even knew the other person was there.

The adage, "It is not what you know, but who you know," was quoted above. It would be more concise if it said: It is what you know, who you know, what the people you know think of you, and your ability to do something with that specific information. Pretend you are the best car salesperson of all time, and you know all the facts about the exact brand of vehicle a referral wants. That information and referral are useless unless you have an automobile to sell them. Your relationships with vendors are as important as your relationships with prospects and centers of influence.

What you know is important. You are only relevant if you are knowledgeable about your product or service in that industry. Life changes fast. To remain valuable and relevant, learn all you can from the best resources you can afford to access.

I helped start a retail trucking insurance agency. I needed more trucking experience. I called an underwriter at a top insurance company. I asked,

"If you were in my position, what would you do?" She replied, "Do you know about MCIEF? Do you know who Tommy Ruke is? You need to." I did not. I looked up the organization "Motor Carrier Insurance Education Foundation." I asked a few others, and they all suggested MCIEF. (This is also an example of phenomenal selling)

The agency joined the organization. MCIEF offered a designation, a type of certification, in trucking. "Trucking Risk Specialist or TRS." Naturally, I signed up. I watched videos, took classes, and found resources.

In the class, I learned much about the industry. That was useful, but it was less insightful than the reminder I received about the importance of relationships.

Tommy Ruke, the founder and CEO of MCIEF, works with Insurance companies, ISO, regulatory agencies, retail agencies, wholesalers, and anyone else who has questions about commercial trucking. Many have said that Tommy is a trucking legend. I would say that Tommy Ruke is trucking insurance. Everyone I spoke to in the industry pointed me to Tommy and MCIEF. The guest speakers and other leaders have genuine respect for this man. (The way others refer to Tommy and the MCIEF is a prime example of phenomenal referral-based sales)

I completed my designation at an in-person training. The classes were what I anticipated that they would be. The difference between them and any other educational seminar I have attended was the openness. Tommy offered everyone in the class the option to have lunch and dinner as a group. We were free to ask him questions and share information. I don't know how many seminars you have attended, but I have been to plenty, and the speaker does not usually share their time or wisdom "off the clock."

What do you think was the overwhelming topic from both Tommy and the guest speakers? Yes, relationships! The trucking industry has just over four-hundred-thousand clients. That is a small number when you consider that there are over four-hundred-thousand insurance agencies across the United States. Everyone stated that without relationships and a reputation for doing quality work, it will be impossible to succeed as trucking insurance agent.

Though, Tommy has made it to a place and reputation where he does not need to prove anything to anyone. At the same time, he invests in everyone. He treated me (bottom of the food chain in trucking insurance) as kindly as he treated the leaders in the industry. Additionally, Tommy, his team, and other leaders shared their contact information to help make the industry better. It is an excellent example of the importance of relationships. It is also an example of leaders developing relationships with people of all levels and skill sets in the industry they lead.

Tommy and the other industry leaders not only set the tone for their platform and the seminar we all attended. He set the example for the attendees that relationships within the community are as meaningful, if not more so. He realized and learned that those who are learning will strive to achieve success with integrity.

Don't Burn Bridges

"If we break up, I will hate you. Everyone I know will hate you, too!" My friend shared that her fiancé said these words to her. Unfortunately, many of us share that sentiment when we stop using a vendor, leave a job, or stop networking with people. It might be that the person wronged you. It might be that you are in different seasons. It might be that your current goals do not align. It may even be that you wronged each other. Whatever the cause, it is better not to burn your bridges. You or they may want to cross back over. People, connections, and companies are valuable. You never know when showing grace, mercy, and forgiveness will benefit you. It doesn't matter how wrong the person was. You have also made mistakes. Jesus said we are supposed to forgive a person 490 times per day. (Matthew 18:22). (That does not mean allowing a person or company to abuse you. My grandmother says, "God didn't create us to be doormats.") Do not throw people away. Do you want to be thrown away when you mess up?

This logic applies to all industries. **Create and maintain healthy relationships. Relationships are a key that starts the vehicle that drives you to success.** (The TRS class featured industry leaders from various roles and all levels of experience and was a great way to blend youth and experience into developing and sharing wisdom within the industry.)

Chapter 5

Coach

Who is the GOAT when it comes to coaching? Did you have a coach (or mentor) who had a positive impact on your life? Athletes become champions because they have a solid personal work ethic and talent to achieve their goals. They also have excellent coaches. We all need champion-minded coaches and mentors. If you do not have one (or several) in your life, get one. I am blessed with many great mentors and coaches. coaches and mentors who positively impact lives are game changers. Use caution when deciding who is allowed to speak into your life.

I took a boxing class in Knoxville, Tennessee. I stood there listening to the coach. I found myself not thinking about boxing. Instead, I wished my sales team could hear this guy. He was good. Really, really good. 'Pay money to sit in an auditorium and listen to good.

We call him Coach or Coach Frank. Frank Eppolito was born in New Jersey. Boxing was a common pastime for kids in his neighborhood. Frank learned to box at an early age. He lived in a neighborhood where a boy needed to know how to defend himself. Frank went into the military, became a two-time national boxing champion and 2011 Ringside World Boxing Champion, a stellar salesman, and a successful car sales team manager. Coach Frank was not the stereotypical car salesman. Later, Coach Frank opened Eppolito's Boxing Gym. He spends his time developing champions. Frank trains professional athletes. He also teaches others who want to think like a champion while getting an amazing workout.

I asked Coach if he would share some thoughts and suggestions about selling, and this is the wisdom he disclosed:

Selling is a huge responsibility to you, your family, your community, and your customer(s). Being phenomenal starts with your state of mind. You must understand who you are and what you want. You will achieve it. Take a good look at yourself. Make positive changes.

Life is bigger than a sale. If you can make the deal without sacrificing your integrity, you are on your way to being phenomenal. Getting to the top is one thing. Staying on top is another. Truthful, honest, sincere, trustworthy, and genuine are the opposite of untruthful, deceptive, and deceitful. "I would rather die on my feet than live on my knees." Euripides. (Good Reads)

I am saying that opportunities for indiscretion, little white lies, or omissions of truth should not easily sway you.

Once you have your mindset right, move on to your health. Stress can destroy you from the inside out. Prioritize your mental, spiritual, and physical health. Get plenty of proper rest, nutrition, and exercise regularly. It will help you to feel great! Your energy flows to your customers. They will feel it and want to be around you. Why are you doing it if you are not happy and energetic while selling? What is selling?

Selling is an action that causes a person, persons, or company to feel, think, and behave in a way that helps everyone to win.

When you are preparing to sell, you will need to develop skills. You must be coachable, be a good listener, be present in the moment, and focus on the person speaking. Acquiring these skills is required of phenomenal salespeople.

Have confidence in yourself, your products, your company or service, and the entire process. Maintain composure in every situation. It is vital to learn to thrive under pressure. Anxiety is not a salesperson's friend. Be calm when needed, and always be passionate.

Believe in yourself and your ability to achieve any skill necessary to get the sale. If you want to close the deal, you must genuinely believe in yourself, your product, and your company. Ensure your hair is presentable, nails are trimmed, shoes are clean, clothing is appropriate, and your breath is fresh. Good hygiene makes you more confident and your customer more comfortable. (You might think worrying about your appearance is dated and unfair. It should not matter how you look. You may be correct, but it is impactful on the sale. It will help if you know what 'appropriate' is. Appropriate varies by industry, audience, and many other factors.)

Keeping the sales process simple has always worked for me. It might be as simple as:

- *Greet your customer. (Set an excellent first impression).*
- *Make eye contact.*
- *Smile big (even if you are on the phone).*
- *Stick out your hand and ask, "May I shake your hand?" (If in person. Once they agree, firmly*

shake their hand. Handshaking rules are a gray area in a post-covid world).

- *If a handshake is inappropriate, a knuckle bump, elbow tap, or nod is fine.*
- *Clearly state your name and title.*
- *Ask for the prospect's name.*
- *Call the prospect by their name during your interaction.*
- *When the prospect speaks, shut up, and listen. (Don't just listen to give a reply, really hear what the person is saying. Listen beyond the words).*
- *Be confident when you speak.*
- *Choose your words wisely and use them to paint a picture.*
- *Ask some easy close-ended questions to get the flow of the conversation started. (Where do you live? Do you have children? etc.).*
- *Move to pre-sell questions (Perhaps these are qualifying questions) – Pre-sell questions should*

be open-ended questions that your prospect cannot answer 'yes' or 'no.'

- *'How' and 'What' are starters for open-ended questions. Do not use "Why." A why question may make a person feel they need to justify their answer.*

- *Uncover the problem. (There is always a problem. The prospect wants a new car, their insurance is too high, they want a bigger house, their computer is too slow, or etc.).*

- *Try to understand their needs and wants. Selling is your job! Take your time.*

- *Solve their problem by getting to 'yes.'*

- *Now that you know what they need and or want and have provided a solution to the problem, you can close the deal.*

- *Build value in your solution and make them feel like they are getting a million-dollar solution to a hundred-dollar problem.*

- *DO NOT use puffy words like 'greatest,' 'number one,' 'best,' or 'worst.'*
- *Explain how the product or service works.*
- *Explain how it will solve the want or need.*
- *Set expectations for how the process will work.*
- *Let them see all the features or benefits of your solution. (For example, if you were a car salesman, anti-lock brakes are a feature, and the advantage of having them is that they help to keep you living."*
- *Close the deal.*
- *Get referrals.*
- *Stay in touch.*

The Close

*The close is where you demonstrate your ability. **Have a great script**! You may amend it as you go, depending on the circumstance. You need to know what you will say as you move into the close. Roleplay to become confident and at ease. Practice,*

practice, practice. Be smooth. Be an expert on your product or service. Have passion and enthusiasm for your product or service.

Validate that your product and customer are a great fit. Do a trial close. Ask: "Are you saying that as long as the terms are agreeable, you are ready to buy it now?" – If they say, "Yes." Then you respond with "Great!" and proceed with close process. If they say "No" or "I'm not prepared to do that today," then ask clarifying questions to determine where you missed a step. Are they worried about the cost? Go back and give them their response to when you discussed that topic earlier. Are they concerned about the product? What concerns do they still have? It may require follow-up responses or simply a review of their earlier answers. They may need reassurance. Worst case, you will need to start over.

Let the prospect relax. If in person, offer them a drink. Start the documentation process. Be thorough, and pay attention to detail, especially the spelling of their name. Do not make sloppy shortcuts. You are the professional.

Go over specifics. Discuss the terms of the deal, item or service options, expectations about the future, and possibly upsell items or services. Ensure that they buy it from you and that you did not 'sell' it to them. You must understand the difference between the two. (The difference is when they 'buy' it from you, it is their choice. As opposed to if you 'sold' it to them, you may have forced the deal or compromised your integrity. Be the person others buy from, not the one selling.)

Being phenomenal does not end with a close. Once you have closed, ask for referrals if it makes sense in your industry. Typically, it does. You could ask, "Are you happy with the work I have done for you?" The customer will typically say 'yes.' Ask them for something specific, "Do you have a friend who needs to replace their car?" "Do you have a relative looking to buy a house?" "Do you have any buddies who are small business owners?" "Do you have a friend with a child turning sixteen?" Or whatever question makes sense for your industry.

Stay in touch with your customer. Make them a customer for life. ("Reach out periodically when you are not trying to make a sale. Keep it short and sweet. It is about showing love." Jena Haynes) It is not easy. If it were, everyone would work in sales.

Many people want the security of an hourly position instead of the opportunities from a performance-based job. You judge, Security versus Opportunity. The money is in opportunities, not security. You create opportunities. It is best to have the freedom to create opportunities instead of letting someone else dictate what you are worth in the name of security.

A key to your success in sales is your belief that you can do it*. Take steps to grow your skills. Do not take no for an answer. (Ziglar, "When People say no, they need to know more") Talk to as many people as possible. Sales have been - and will always be - a game of numbers. The more presentations I make, the* *more I will sell. There are many ways to find prospects and prequalify leads.*

Sales can be brutal to your feelings, emotions, and everything else down to your soul. Rejection happens. Expect it. Be prepared for it. Remember, it is a numbers game. You must hear "No" to get to the "tell me more cases" and eventually to the "Yes." Prequalification and technology help to increase the closing ratio.

***It will be a battle;** **you must have the heart of a champion fighter.** Refuse to be defeated. Train your mind: No quit, no retreat, no surrender!*

I can! I will! I must! That is how you think every single day. You will give 100% of yourself. It is one of the hardest things you will do because you not only fight circumstances, but you are fighting your weaknesses.

*Understand that every great warrior had the urge to quit, but they refused to stop. **The warrior mindset requires discipline, controlling your*** *thoughts, and what you allow into your mind.* *What you see and think is often what you manifest.*

Do not always be looking up. What I mean is, pause to see those around you who have less than you - mentally, physically, and emotionally. Think about those who don't have the ability you have to create opportunities. Think about those who don't have the capacity for sales. Think about how blessed you are to be able to do what you do. Appreciate your blessings. You won't have to look far to see that it could be worse.

If selling gets heavier than you thought, take your mind back to what you are grateful for. ***Gratitude will pull you through difficult times so you can achieve your goals****. Making time to serve others is a great way to keep your head straight.*

Many people are counting on you. You matter. You got this. ***There comes a time in your life when you cross the ropes, step into the ring, and do your best. You can rest the results in peace. You*** *may not win every round, but you will win the bout.*

— Coach Frank Eppolito

Coach Frank demands his athletes behave with respect for themselves and others. Sportsmanship is always required. Sportsmanship and respect are equally important in sales careers.

Chapter 6
Scales of Success

How is it that some people accomplish exponentially more than others? There are 24 hours each day, 365 days each year. Is it the use of systems, technology, and time management? These factors play a part. These alone will not tip the scales. The only way companies and people achieve largescale success is by leveraging the power of other people.

Erin Cooper understands the power of people. She decided to become a realtor in 2016. She knew she was a capable salesperson, but talent alone was not enough. Erin spent a lot of time developing her system and learning the industry. She is a big believer in time-blocking and used it to organize her days. Today Erin is the founder of the Cooper Group as well as the president of a local realty office. One major key to her success is the team she built.

To achieve large-scale success, you cannot do it with your two hands. You create infrastructure and then build a team to run the infrastructure. When you establish your team, do not tell them they did a fantastic job if they did not. If necessary, discipline them when they need it. Do not hesitate to start at the bottom if you are new to the game or switching industries. Foundations are crucial to stability.

The greatest of all leaders builds other leaders. Jesus of the Bible would also agree. He made disciples and told them to make other disciples. It is a tenant of how the world works.

William Arrowood Jr., and his family, built an empire of insurance-related companies across the United States. I was asking for his advice. It was with great excitement in his eyes that he gave me advice. Then, he told me about a project he had coming up. I said, "You have been working non-stop your whole life. You do not need money. When is enough - enough?" He was startled by my question. But he answered, "It is not about the money." He is a gamesman who enjoys the conquest. Capitalism is part of his identity.

When it comes to communication, the main thing is to ask open-ended questions. Then, listen-listen-listen.

Find a mentor or coach. Read about your industry. Try to understand what works and how others in your field have achieved success. Learn everything that you can learn. Be clear about your wants and needs. Embrace technology. Know what you want to accomplish as the sales professional you choose to be.

Networking

The scales of success are tipped in your favor when you learn the art of networking. **The art of networking is simple: be at ease meeting people anytime, anywhere.** My main thought on networking is to go out and do it consistently. If you get to know others, participate in their groups, and show up for them. Relationships will come, along with the trust you build. Be patient. When you network it is important to smile, listen, show interest, learn, and be engaged in the moment.

Good networkers produce referrals. Strong networking skills are a way to make you phenomenal.

Visit several kinds of groups. Find groups that offer the culture you want. Find a group that pushes you out of your comfort zone. Diversity is a good thing. Find a group that inspires you. Find a group where most of the people at the table are more accomplished than you think you are. You never want to be the brightest, most successful person at the table.

Never judge a group based on price. I am fortunate to be part of BPPA. (Business Professionals Prayer Association) It is a free association. BPPA has professionals who share my worldview, faith, and hunger for professional development. The Bible says, "Iron sharpens Iron" (Proverbs 27:17). There is value in finding both like-minded groups and groups that oppose your worldview. There is beauty in the challenges that help us understand one another. There is merit to showing love and respect to those who don't share our perspective.

Referrals

I encouraged you to build your network by inspiring connections to send you 'their people.' Getting referrals is tricky. It used to be that when you closed a sale, you would say something along the lines of, "Did I do a good job for you?" and when the client said "Yes," you would say, "Then please give me the names of 10 of your friends and family members so I can do a good job for them, too." I was never good at using that method, but I found a method that worked for me.

At one time, all my sales were coming from referrals. It was wonderful! Referrals for me have happened in a few ways:

- **Organic** - where a client or friend told someone else to call me.

- **Centers of Influence** - I developed a relationship with a center of influence, and they had their clients call me. An example of this is, as an insurance agent, mortgage brokers would have their clients call me when looking for homeowner's insurance. Centers of Influence was my favorite way to get referrals. **Who do you know that has contacts who want to buy what you have to sell?**

- **Mention It** - Another way that worked well for me was casually saying, "Remember me when someone mentions they need insurance."

- **Drip Marketing** - Use drip marketing. Drip marketing keeps you on top of someone's mind.

- **Gift Cards**. Use to offer referral gift cards. Find gift card compliance rules for your industry.

To gain referrals, design a system that works for you. The method you build will depend on and vary within your industry, personality, and others. Try a variety of options and focus on the ones that work best. Contrary to some of the advice you will receive, there is no such thing as "the best way."

Discovering what works for you is always okay. 3M had a slogan that said, "We do not make a lot of the products you buy; we make a lot of the products you buy better." Apply that slogan to referrals. Turn good into better by crafting your process of acquiring referrals.

These are some of the ways you will measure or gauge your success.

Chapter 7
King Of Your Emotions (KOYE)

"Be the best salesperson ever in ten easy steps!"; "You can make it rain!"; "Picture yourself as number one!"; "Think it, be it, do it!"; "You can!"

One-liners are great, but they are not the star of this show. It is no secret that people often buy based on emotion.

Do you realize that you are also selling based on emotion? If you are human, you are. Emotions are bussin (extra good)! We are not here to tell you to squash your feelings or lose your passion. We are here to tell you to become the King of Your Emotions. (KOYE). Being the King of Your Emotions is the best way to prevent yourself from getting hooked on a feelin'. Emotions are an incredible help.

How do you feel when you close a big sale? How do you feel when you complete a challenging deal? How do you feel when you win any client? How is your mood if you have a bad sales day, week, month, or quarter? How does your mood impact your life? How do life events change your ability to sell?

If you are like most people, I can answer the questions for you. Closing a big sale is exhilarating. Closing a challenging sale can make you feel like a champion strategist! (Insert theme song from the Rocky movies) Even if that difficult sale didn't produce the projected revenue. Closing any sale is a good feeling.

Any time sales are slow, you feel like you are losing the game. Or it can make you determined to come out swinging. Slow sales are a mood squasher.

Pay for sales is generally tied to individual performance. Some would argue that lost income when sales are in a downturn is a cause of depression. Perhaps there is some validity to that. I argue that it is more than that. Sales mood is about the insatiable competitive spirit that salespeople have living inside them. If someone has not learned to be KOYE (King of your emotions), their sales will directly reflect their what is happening in thier personal life.

Have you ever played video games? I tried playing "Nintendo's Super Mario Bros the Mission to Save the Princess." I was terrible at it. It annoyed me that I did not understand what the reward was for a completed the mission. It wasn't clearly defined, so I lost interest. (**Many salespeople lose interest when their commission or pay structure is unclear**.)

My best friend, Julie's, brother was a different story. Whenever I went to her house, I noticed he played video games for hours. One day while I was there, he shouted, "I'm about to save the princess!" We ran into his room to watch him. He did indeed save the princess. I will never forget the disappointment I felt when he saved Princess Peach. Nothing happened! He did not get an award. There was no title. Nothing! I asked, "What now?" He said,

"I start over on a new mission." (Salespeople often need recognition as much as they need money. Recognition provides reassurance of performance.)

It was a complete and utter letdown. A few years later, I was working as an insurance agent. I had what I thought was a lofty goal. And I knocked it out of the park! Suddenly, the feeling I had when my friend's brother rescued Princess Peach returned. "Now what?"

Sales joy is addictive, and like any drug, the pleasure is fleeting. It does not last long. Another problem is that **it doesn't feel how you think it will feel.** It always feels better in your imagination.

If you are going to become KOYE (King of Your Emotions), you will need to set realistic expectations for how things will feel. Even when you do, making sales is still addictive. The endorphins in your brain create a "rush" when you close a deal. Like any addiction, it leaves you wanting another high. Think, plan, and reason beyond that high.

To some, sales are like caffeine, chocolate, or sugar. To others, selling is like meth, cocaine, or other drugs. Salespeople often earn a reputation for having addictive tendencies and struggling with monogamy. I am sure there are multiple reasons why.

My guess is: time away from family, existing mental health traits, the need for energy, the hunger to stay on high, etc. The main thing that sales-related addictions say is that too many salespersons have never learned to become KOYE. (King of Your Emotions)

Part of becoming King of Your Emotions is knowing who you are. Know what and how much you desire to achieve and earn. You can aim for a monetary number or declare an objective. (For example, Bob's goal is to make $450,000 annually. Amy's goal is to earn enough to cover all expenses, provide for her family, and still have time to relax. Jan's goal is to be number one in her region)

Sales, like coffee, are a wonderful thing. It can also be the thing that controls your entire life.

That is why there are tons of folks who would be outstanding salespeople who quit before their career ever gets started. They do not like the rollercoaster of emotions, can't take the constant pressure, or don't want their life controlled by their work. (These are people who did not know they could become KOYE)

I used to tell my son, "You don't have to be the best as long as you do your personal best" He corrected me by saying: "I don't want to do my personal best at everything." He was talking about school. He was a gifted student, but he refused to take advanced classes. He enjoyed not having homework. He liked his free time. My son chose to be the student he was. You are the sales professional you decide to be.

Part of being KOYE (King of Your Emotions), is realizing that you control your choices. You do not have to go as hard as possible. You go as far as you choose to go.

Having systems and processes to follow will help you stay out of your emotions. Always follow the process and not your feelings. When in doubt, get advice on the matter. Experts and mentors are there for a reason. There is no shame in asking for help.

Ephesians 4:26-32 teaches not to be led by emotions. Jeremiah 17:9 teaches that our hearts are deceitful above all things. Proverbs 28:26 tells us that if we trust only in ourselves, we are a fool.

It is a lot like piloting a plane. Pilots must trust the instruments and not their sight. To become KOYE (King of Our Emotions) we must outsell our emotions.

Mental health issues really exist. I do not think there are any readymade answers for complex problems. As a believer in Christ, my first answer is always prayer. As a mother who raised a child with PTSD Bi-Polar, I learned the value of mental health professionals. At times, seeking wise counsel is part of becoming KOYE.

Do not take things personally. You never know what another person might be going through. Perhaps, the call dropped, or the person was short with you because they had things going on that were unrelated to you.

Develop GRIT! (Angela Duckworth's book, Grit, is an excellent read and is on the suggested reading.) Have determination and keep going. You will only succeed in sales if you have grit. I thought I had it until I met my team in Ukraine. We were in a video meeting. Ellen's screen went dark. I asked if there was a problem. She said, "No, it was a missile, it is impacting the electricity. We can continue." I offered to wait. Ellen insisted, "No, we will continue now." (I was "shook" and I was a world way. She refused to lose focus.) Ellen has next level grit! Do you have grit? Emotions do not control people who have grit. It is hard when family or life interfere. We are not saying you must ignore your reality. Quite the opposite, we are saying if you have grit, realize what's going on and practice self-care.

Chapter 8

Sales Tips and Tricks

What was the best sales tip or wisdom nugget you have ever received? Proverbs in the Bible was an entire book of tips or wisdom nuggets. I am comparing this chapter to the book of Proverbs. The book of Proverbs has lots of random advice. This chapter is random advice for the salesperson.

- Money does not equal peace or joy.

- Poverty is not a badge of honor. Don't be ashamed of success.

- Forgive others.

- Know your weaknesses (You have some).

- King of your emotions (be the KOYE).

- Perseverance is crucial.

- Have mentors.

- Read daily.

- Failure leads to success.

- If you never fail, you will not learn how to fix mistakes.

- Learn the rules of whatever it is you are selling.

- Set effective boundaries.

- Know who you are, be you.

- Know what you want.

- Know how much of it you want.

- Learn how to get what you want.

- Create an action plan.

- Be realistic.

- Be empathetic.

- Listen, educate – Do not give orders.

- Prepare to be interrupted.

- Create a positive sales environment (Think Feng Shui).

- Time blocking works.

- If you have A.D.D., color blocking and creating small tasks will help.

- The Bible says the laborer is worthy of the hire. Bring honor to whoever hires you.

Plants and Storms

Endure hardships. Allow your teams to experience and endure hardships as well. I decided to raise tomato plants. I bought seeds and planted them. They came up quickly and were growing well. They were about three inches tall and began to have trouble standing. I called my grandmother. I said, "I do not know what is wrong. I kept them inside, protected them from the weather, and took care of everything." She said, "You are the problem! The plants need the wind and the rain. It is the storms and the weather that makes them strong. They need to learn to stand on their own."

We need to learn to face storms. It will make us stronger.

Sales at the Flea Market

I notice how salespeople behave everywhere I go. I love seeing potential in people and learning from them. It is instinctive at this point in my career. I stopped at a small flea market. I lost all interest in looking at vegetables. I became captivated by the sales styles I was observing.

There was a man there who had nice-looking vegetables. He was clean, quiet, and sitting in a chair. I wanted to buy from him. I couldn't get his attention and didn't know his vegetables' price.

Some vendors were loud, calling out to customers as they walked by, trying to engage them so they could draw them into their shops.

Others clearly marked prices with colored markers on cardboard signs above each of the kinds of vegetables. They were not calling out to people but were pleasant when people stopped. They had more visitors than both other booths combined.

The quiet man had the best-looking vegetables. But he did nothing to engage his customers and needed signage. He got the least amount of traffic. The best product had the least amount of traffic.

It isn't always about how good you are, but how well you present the product, and the cost of that product, that matters.

Salesman Psychology

People often get caught up in the emotional game tied to an item. My former father-in-law, LA, had a yard sale when his wife passed away. She had an antique dog. LA had the dog outside with his yard sale items. A gentleman came to buy it. My father-in-law offered a price, and the gentleman said, "That is too much!" They went back and forth for quite some time. My father-in-law, LA, was tired of the game, and he said, "It is not for sale anymore. I am taking it back in the house." The man tried to give him three times the original price. It was a brilliant strategy for my father-in-law until he refused to sell the antique dog. My father-in-law lost himself to the sales game, or maybe he won.

Restaurant servers are salespersons. You know this if you are a server. Do you want dessert?

You worked hard this week; you deserve a dessert! Can I bring you another drink? How about an app? Did you see our special? Man, I hear good things about that new entrée! One more round? There are times sales organizations seek out servers because they have grit. Servers are actively selling every day. Do not take these workers for granted. Tip them well and show them respect. It is a craft as much as whatever it is you are offering.

It is easier to talk to people if you do not spew jargon from your industry. Use the words your prospect would use if talking to a friend. (Try to talk to people on an eighth-grade level. It is not condescending. It doesn't matter how intellectual your prospect or client is. If you use words about your industry that any eighth grader could understand, the conversation will flow smoothly. Other professionals don't want to have to learn your terminology.) It is also better if you sound friendly. Set the tone, but do not be bossy. Be assertive, not aggressive. Control the conversation but be sweet.

Ask for the sale. Get a resolution or set the next step. Continuously develop the relationship.

Follow your instincts. If something feels off, it usually is. I worked on an account in Newport, Tennessee, a few years ago. It felt off. I did not know why. I followed the procedure, and I asked all the questions. I even called the underwriter. I knew something was wrong. (There are times you just know.) I started to decline the risk. I argued with myself. I convinced myself I was being foolish. A couple of weeks later, the house I insured was a total fire loss. Fraud investigators found out that the insured had a similar commercial loss. Our questionnaire did not ask about commercial losses, and the report didn't show commercial claims. I believe to this day that the fire was intentional. **Trust your instincts!**

Communication Style

Be willing and able to communicate on every platform. Use whatever means of communication the prospect or client prefers. I know it can be scary. Yes, it is vital to honor privacy and compliance rules. Technology will allow you to add text messaging or a plethora of other applications to whatever sales management system you use. Many of my clients use a mix of communication mediums. Update your soft skills. It is not about what makes you comfortable. It is about what gives you a competitive edge.

Stop with the Horse and Pony Show

Going all the way around a mountain to make the prospect fall in love with your product or service and prove that they would be foolish to choose anyone or anything other than what you have, is ineffective. It is condescending, and you are not the only game in town. Get to your point. Stop wasting people's time. Share the relevant information and let the prospect make an informed decision. If you were selling "red bottom" shoes, you would not spend hours building them up or trying to find a way to justify their costs. No, they cost what they cost. If your product is expensive, own up to that. Apple has never apologized for selling $1200 phones. Sneakerheads do not regret the price they pay for Retro Jordans. You do not walk into a Ferrari dealership looking for Honda prices.

Consumers and business-to-business clients understand the game. When they do not, they consult the internet. Be real, prompt, efficient, and get to the point! Give consumers solid facts. Know how to educate them. Go beyond a simple web search.

We recently viewed and tried out many software companies. I knew which one I wanted to go with. It is best-in-class, and it had above-average pricing.

As we got into the demo with the vendor that I wanted to use the sales team would not relent from the horse and pony show. I told them multiple times that it was not necessary.

They continued through their process for such an extended period that I no longer wanted to buy from them. They ignored me. Remember to pause your plan long enough to hear what the client or prospect tells you. People will teach you how to win their business when you listen.

Get over yourself!

Prospects can find another way to get the product or service you offer. They will buy from whoever works the way they want to work and makes them feel how they want to feel so long as the cost is reasonable.

Learn about the prospect and how you can help them by fulfilling their needs. They will respond to someone interested in helping them. Find out what they need. Commit. Ask. Observe. Put yourself in their shoes.

Be Indispensable

Learn to be indispensable. Be willing to do what no one else is doing. I do not mean to violate ethics or morals. Please do not go there with this advice.

I met an African IT engineer at a coffee shop. He told a story of how when he was trying to gain favor with a company, he noticed there was a need for a compliance policy. It was outside of his regular services, but he was a compliance expert. He did the compliance service for free with no strings attached. Today, the large company he gave it to values him greatly as their representative.

Ginny, a sales representative, came to the ribbon cutting of our newest location. She found a way to connect with me and others at the event.

Ginny followed up for a subsequent meeting by sending me a thank you email and some potential leads. She was not pushy, but ensured we knew who she was.

Her competition did not attend the ribbon cutting but requested a meeting with us. The counterpart was selling. It was like she took a page from the fictional 1980s book on sales that I referenced earlier. The two competitors had similar products and costs. I chose Ginny because she was engaged and focused on relationship building.

Investigate

Be prepared. Do an internet search of your clients and prospects before creating your proposals. Look at their personal social media and business platforms as well as websites.

Search your own name. Prospects are checking you and your competition out as well. Run a few quick searches to see what the internet says about you.

Politics & Religion

Do you want to exercise your freedom of speech and post whatever you think or feel on social platforms? If so, do it, but be ready to be judged for it as well.

Prospects, clients, potential sales employers, and others are checking you out. They will know exactly where you stand. Your personal views may cost you clients or help you gain them. Politics, behaviors, bias, and other things impact hiring, firing, and buying decisions. On a corporate level, they may have a policy that swears it does not matter. When it comes down to it, most of the time, your politics, or lack thereof, matter.

These days I keep my nose out of public politics. My social posts are things I do not mind the whole world seeing or knowing about me. I call that hanging a lantern on it. I do share openly about my faith as a Christian. I have lost and gained opportunities because of it.

Share or do not share. It is your choice. You will be judged in the law of opinion based on the bias of whoever sees the post.

Consider all communications made on the internet as public for the whole world, even if you meant for it to only go to one or a group of friends.

Summary

This book is to help you think outside of the basic parameters of business and sales. If you are a salesperson and have behaviors that need to be corrected, correct them.

If you are a manager training 'dated ideas' or dated technology, stop it. Update your process, and ensure you have the current information, technology, and strategies available for you and your team to succeed. Then, train!

If you are new to the sales industry, and after reading this, you still want to be in sales, good for you! Excellent salespeople are needed. Every champion is told how hard it would be, how unlikely their success is, and why it would be much easier to quit.

Go into sales with your eyes open. You should be free misconceptions or ideas of grandeur. If you understand that there are difficulties and pitfalls, yet something within you is burning. You can do this! You can achieve your goals.

Once you decide within yourself how much of the sales pie you want in the season of life that you are in. It is yours and ready for the taking. Go get it!

There is an adage in ministry that says, "Ministry would be easy were it not for the people." That is also true of sales. Sales would buy easy were it not for the buyers." Jesus was perfect in every way, and people crucified him for his efforts. There will be days that even when you have done your best, you will feel persecuted and unappreciated. Some buyers are impossible to please. Keep doing good, anyway.

I took over a book of business for a Mr. Lloyd Burton, his life-long excellence was evident in his files and with his clients. Not everyone will love you, but you will earn respect when you consistently work hard with integrity.

Be the sales professional that you choose to be. Great salespeople are not born – they are made. (Ziglar) Greatness is a choice. You can let the opportunity to be a salesperson control you, or you can control it.

After all, living your dreams should be non-negotiable. Living your dreams is possible if you don't get hooked on a feelin'.

Suggested Reading

The Bible

<u>Sales 101</u> – Zig Ziglar

(Anything and everything by Zig Ziglar)

<u>Grit</u> – Angela Duckworth

<u>Unbroken</u> – Laura Hillenbrand

<u>Rainmaker</u> – Jeffrey J Fox

<u>Goliath Must Fall</u> – Louie Giglio

<u>Make Your Dreams Bigger than Your Memories</u> - Terrie Savelle Foy

<u>The Wedge</u> – Randy Schwantz

<u>Taking Flight</u> – Jeff Cochran

<u>Don't Get Hooked on a Feelin'</u> – Teresa Sheppard

References

Bible Gateway. (n.d.). NIV. Retrieved 2022, from
Bible Gateway:
https://www.biblegateway.com/passage/?sea
rch=Genesis%2014&version=NIV

Duckworth, A. (n.d.). *GRIT* .

Foy, T. S. (n.d.). Retrieved 02 04, 2023, from
https://www.bing.com/videos/search?q=terri
+savelle+foy+live+your+dreams&view=det
ail&mid=8ED30EB73779F22BE9D68ED30
EB73779F22BE9D6&FORM=VIRE

Good Reads. (n.d.). Retrieved 02 04, 2023, from
https://www.goodreads.com/quotes/11795-i-
would-rather-die-on-my-feet-than-live-on

Harvard Business Review. (n.d.). *When Quiet
Quitting Is Worse Than the Real Thing*.
Retrieved February 04, 2023, from
https://hbr.org/2022/09/when-quiet-quitting-
is-worse-than-the-real-thing

Pew Research . (2022, August 14). *Reference.com* .
Retrieved from

https://www.reference.com/world-view/percentage-world-christian-4baefda21d3bfcfd

Psychology Today. (n.d.). What Motivates Sexual Promiscuity. Retrieved 02 04, 2023, from https://www.psychologytoday.com/us/blog/evil-deeds/201111/what-motivates-sexual-promiscuity

Ziglar, Z. (n.d.). Retrieved 02 04, 2023, from https://www.youtube.com/watch?v=ApWjzPCskLc

Notes: